BEFORE WHOSE GLORY

Lawrence Kessenich

FUTURECYCLE PRESS

Mineral Bluff, Georgia

Published by FutureCycle Press
Mineral Bluff, Georgia, USA

ISBN 978-1-938853-11-1

Contents

For Janet,
who taught me to love life
and for
Laura and Charlie,
whom I love more than life itself

PERMEABLE BORDERS

Angelus

For Mena

In Campania, at her grandfather's farm,
fieldstone house secure as a castle,
she sleeps beneath the high eaves underhung
with swallows' nests like pots of clay.

She walks the vineyards with him, too small
to see over the vines, her eyes full of leaves,
fat grapes and, overhead, the bellies
and wings of birds about their business.

She longs to see the birds, to be the birds.
He lifts her high to look into their nests
at perfect oval eggs, at hatchlings
scrawny, pink and vulnerable.

When he arises to work the fields, barking
dogs wake her. She listens to the newborn
swallows just outside her shutters crying
for their breakfast with the dawn.

From her bed, she stares up at the vaulted
ceiling, at the painted angel flying around
the light fixture, naked save the loincloth
rippling across his muscular thighs.

His wings are white as a swallow's belly
and from a basket on his arm he strews
flowers across a faux sky, each growing
brighter as the sun outside rises higher.

Finally, she throws off the covers,
pulls the shutters open. Sunlight
like a hundred chandeliers bathes
the angel in glory and herself in joy.

Love: A Journey

Somewhere west of Minneapolis, black clouds
seal off the sky above the dome car, where
we've come to distract ourselves from our latest
quarrel. Desperate to avoid talking, we stuff

our mouths with trail mix (packed to save
the cost of bad Amtrak food) and read our books.
Night comes, and with it a biblical
midsummer storm. Rain hammers the glass

above our heads. Lightning plunges
like a knife into the earth, illuminates
the flat plains of North Dakota, transforming
them into vast, dark lakes of fire. Eventually,

the thrumming of the rain puts us to sleep.
At dawn, I wake to a dreamscape, an ocean
of tall grass waving over swells of hills
tinged pink by rising sun. Maria is

asleep beside me, her Botticelli
Venus face in repose, the worried crease
between her eyes smoothed. Just then,
a herd of tawny antelope appear

outside the window, lope gracefully over
the soft rise of my heart, disappear behind it.

Love: A Misconception

The spring moon rose like a promise
over Lake Michigan, a transparent
orb in which we read our future. You
would capture the world inside
the black box of your Nikon. I
would do the same with words.

Kneeling on the damp sand, all we saw
was possibility. Rays of moonshine
laid a path across the still water;
we imagined following it over
the event horizon into our dreams.

Only later would we kneel before each other,
begging understanding and mercy.
Only later would we learn that
moonshine also burns like kerosene.

Only later would we discover the true definition
of event horizon: "the surface of a black hole;
a point of no return; anything within it
can't get out, even at the speed of light."

Meditating with a Dog Named Vasana*

The mind is not easily ignored.
Told to sit in the corner like
a good little dog, he disobeys,
bringing thoughts like toys:
a green rubber block, a stuffed squirrel,
an old, slimy, gnawed-over bone.

Take this simple mantra, I tell him,
and play with that. But he wants to do more.
He barks, licks my face, sniffs my crotch,
drops a brightly colored ball at my feet.
Vasana! I say sharply.
But to no avail. He is my dog
and requires my attention.

I toss his ball across the room
again and again and again.
He brings it back to me
again and again and again
until, finally, he drops it,
lays down in his corner, and falls asleep,
dreaming of sticks thrown into rivers.
Good dog, Vasana. Good dog.

*Sanskrit for experiential impressions that cause mental fluctuations

The Artisan

An idle mind is the devil's workshop.

I picture him up there, having made
himself tiny to fit in, but no less
formidable for that. He has removed
his stylish black cape and hung it carefully.
He sits at an ebony work table,
silk sleeves rolled back neatly to reveal
the hands of a jeweler with which
he fashions a tiny temptation—
a ruby of rage, perhaps, or a
glittering diamond of avarice.
Though small, his pieces have been known
to light up an entire room or
erupt like long-dormant volcanoes.
He never takes a vacation, but
on lazy days he bangs out lozenges
of lust in bold carnelian,
inexpensive pieces
he can always count on.

Middle Age Spring

After weeks of dripping,
wet blanket clouds, spring lights up—
blue skies that won't quit, flowers
opening suddenly, like children
bursting through doors.

I help clean refuse from
the banks of the Charles, find
a shard of Chinese teapot
with fluttering bluebirds,
a used condom accompanied
by the one-shot bottles of
Smirnoff that inspired
its use, a dirty old white
pillow that turns out to be
the upturned breast of a dead goose.

Later, my wife and I slide out
the sunporch windows, remove
winter's grime, invite
the sun back in. For supper
we eat scampi, wish we'd
bought lime for gin-and-tonics.
Instead, I use the last finger
of whisky in ginger ale, bidding
farewell to our winter drink.

Even at bedtime, it's
too warm to close the windows.
Naked under a sheet,
I listen to the foreign
yet familiar sounds of cars
passing below the window,
teenagers talking excitedly
in the park across the street.
I miss the tucked-in quiet

of winter, but a young place
in my heart has opened
with the flowers
and will not close.

Emergency Call

*An Oregon woman was arrested for misusing
911 when she called and asked for "the cutest cop
I've ever seen" to return to her house.*

If that wasn't an emergency,
I'd like to know what is: ten months
without sex, the kids at camp,
a hot summer day smelling
of tanning oil and ripe flowers,
when this god appears,
all black curls and blue eyes,
his incandescent smile
melting my legs like ice cream.
There really *was* an intruder
poking around in the
back yard, but my god found
nothing disturbed, except me,
mooning at him like a lovesick
cow. And then he was leaving me,
saying don't hesitate to
call again if need be. And so
I did. Perhaps I should have
mentioned the intruder again,
but he was long gone from
my mind, replaced by muscles,
blue cotton and a smile
that wouldn't quit.

Brief Vacation

As I wash dishes on an overcast day
miles from the Atlantic, wind from the East
unexpectedly delivers the sea to my window
like an invitation to Cape Cod. The briny odor
conjures waves falling over themselves
to get to shore, sandpipers motoring
up the sand to avoid them, the muffled
cries of children breasting cold surf.
My neighbor's house has fallen away,
revealing in the blue-gray distance
a sailboat's silhouette on the horizon,
the steamy spout of a whale. I breathe
deeply, hands submerged in water,
fill my lungs with an ocean of air.

Enlightenment

Everything depends upon
our comprehending physics.
How the fat man's thigh
pressed against yours
on the bus seat is
your thigh, too. How

the crazy woman's mumbled
"God help me" is from
your lips as well. How
the warm bread smell
of a sleeping child's hair
unites with your olfactory

nerves. The borders
are permeable, the energy
exchange liquid and continuous.
We breathe the dust of million-
year-old galaxies, trade atoms
with a clutched stone.

Death Wish

On the twisted streets of Baghdad
drills whirl like demon dervishes,
spouting blood from living skulls.
The jagged snows of Afghanistan
bristle with tribal rifles. Suicide
bombers bloom bloody roses
in the markets of Jerusalem.
It is a world with teeth bared,
claws at the ready, a world
to hide from or pretend
does not exist, a misbegotten
world, whether formed by God
or Nature. Perhaps it's time
to admit it's all gone wrong,
end this failed experiment,
sweep the shards of broken
test tubes from the laboratory
table, watch them glitter through
the air like dying stars.

Consolation

Out beneath a bridal veil of stars, you yearn
for consummation, long to sweep a billion
tiny fires into embrace. You have to settle for
my arm across your shoulders.

What can I tell you?
You are lonely as a star crossing the void,
but so is each of us. The blaze that lights
your heart twinkles only faintly to that Lover
waiting billions of miles away.

You want each moment to be an embrace,
but even you could not relieve the world's loneliness.
It is part of us, like arms and legs. We spend
our lives attempting to reunite in small
and often brutal ways, but we are whispering
through an endless dark and no one hears.

If we are one, the knowledge is buried so deep
that we no longer feel it, except in these
brief moments when the sky folds back
and drops the stars into our lap.

Primordial

In the foothills of the Alps, Jungfrau's
promontory brooding over the valley,
I diverge from the road, plow through
knee-deep snow up a hillside park, then,
winded, rest on a buried bench, listen

to my ragged breath grow slowly
smooth and quiet. I hear the
fabled sound of one hand clapping,
the round, seductive sound of silence—
beingness, nothingness, the mother

of everything, the world before it
was born, an impulse in the unconscious
of God. Into that silence, my constricted

heart expands. I simply am, I need only
be. Silence, the bosom of existence,
nurtures me. Silence rocks me in its arms,
dissolves my pain and doubt. Silence sings
a lullaby that, if allowed, would

put me to sleep forever…happily. Then,
from far across the valley, a chainsaw
groans to life, and just below the hill
a dog barks, a child cries, a train
creaks into Grindelwald.

EVEN THE BIGGEST FAMILY

Walking Home from Work

The moon is cold, the sky
cerulean blue. Mars and
Venus, close as lovers all
week, move apart, estranged.

Walking home, I wander through
a hilltop cemetery
past a newly filled grave,
soil sinking at the edges.

High in the sky, Orion,
his belt cinched tightly from
winter privations, watches
my progress indifferently.

I've had lonely nights when
he would have been a savior,
but this night my wife and
children await me with
hot food and open arms,
perhaps even a fire
to take away the chill.

This is why the world grows
cold: so we can warm it up.
This is why the sky goes
dark: so we can light it.
This is why we all leave
home: so we can return.

The hero's journey is
out and back, from cold to
warmth, from dark to light.
Each week, we are heroic
in our own little ways;
each week we deserve
a hero's welcome home.

One-Sided Conversation

He, the one with cancer, is passed around
on a cell phone, retelling his tale
like the Ancient Mariner. His albatross
is white, too—the innocent-looking cells
flock in the ocean of his body,
feed on his organs as if they were
a school of fish. He would like us
to relieve him, but even the biggest family
cannot lift this burden from his neck.
We can only bear witness to his drama
enacted under the narrow
proscenium of his ribs, can only be
the audience he so desperately desires.

Fatal Insomnia

Fatal familial insomnia is a rare brain disease
where the patient loses the ability to fall asleep.

Ambition is the first to go. The bright
platitudes that get us out of bed each day
ring hollow with no bed to leave,
no reassuring sleep with which to
burnish them. They recede into the
void like distant stars. Human faces
turn to water before your bleary eyes,
mirages speaking nonsense. All
you want is to escape the endless
headache of consciousness, the dull
throb of thoughts. Slowly, your body goes
slack, unable to initiate
even the smallest movements. Death
becomes a lover longed for, but
not easily won. He watches
from the corner, smiling pitilessly
as your life seeps out. And only when
the last drop has been drained does he
step forward to claim the shell
of your wasted body.

The Cuban in the Basement

He used to teach them Spanish,
Sally, Jack and a few neighbors.
He had a day job, then, but not
being the sort to compromise
told his *loco* boss something
unpleasant about the boss's mother.
Now he lives with them, gets up
each day, puts on a white shirt
and tie, eats Wheaties and
walks off into the world.
Over dinner he regales them
with stories of compromises
not made, puffing out his chest
and lapsing into rapid
Spanish neither of them can
follow. When they have wine
he drinks too much and sings
to Sally. They should probably
ask him to go, but his proud
refusal to conform inspires
them to confront their own crazy
bosses, stopping just short
of insulting the bosses' mothers.

General Grandma

I see them on the river path daily,
a wiry Chinese woman in khakis
and a bucket hat wielding a stick
with which she prods two overweight
grandsons, exhorting them to walk
faster. Both boys wear backpacks
freighted with bricks from the border
of grandma's garden, their puffy round
faces red with exertion. When I pass by,
grandma waves at me and smiles
but then returns to the task at hand,
setting the pace for her charges,
who look as if they regret being
drafted into the army of her family.

Mute

"Can't speak" scrawls the silver-tongued
Galway poet on the Gresham Hotel pad
his wife produces from her purse
with a St. Patrick's Purgatory pencil.
His letters zigzag across the paper
like lines on a lie-detector graph.

When he'd written that Trinity coed's
number on the pad in Dublin, three weeks
before, his hand was steady as a surgeon's.
The pencil was Marion's, from her annual
pilgrimage to Lough Derg, where she did
her damnedest to pray him out of hell.

This was hell on earth, the words he normally
declaimed knotting like old ropes in his mouth.
His mind was arthritic hands, painfully
attempting to untie the words, throw
lifelines out into the sterile room.
Marion just stared at him blankly.

What was he without his golden voice,
a voice one critic called the megaphone
of heaven? He was a cathedral bell without
its clapper, the bull horn of a gelded bull,
the Dublin Symphony Orchestra
all dressed up and no place to play.

Just writing the words "Can't speak"
on the pad had been a trial, but not to
be able to speak them—his tongue clumsy
as a sledge hammer in the hands of
a boy—was more than he could bear.
Marion handed back the pad.

He wanted to confess, to beg her
forgiveness. Without his voice,

she was all he had. He could only
speak through her now, her low husky
tones promising to lend his bombastic
words an unfamiliar subtlety and grace.

Daniel Boone Speaks to His Wife

Do you think I like facing it
alone out there in the legless
forest? Don't you know that fear
steals over me each night with
the creeping shadows? If I could
be a man any other way
I would do it, but I am
more afraid of the store clerk's
bland apron and the stinking
breath of the saloon keeper's
patrons. I'd rather wrestle
a bear than a gunny sack
full of sugar or a drunk.
The lonely wilderness is my
burden and my joy. I converse
with the animals who don't
try to kill me—and sometimes
with those that do—their dying
growls more eloquent than the
preacher's fine words. I was born
to bathe alone beneath a falls,
not in the tepid water of
a tin tub. And if I can only
come home to you a few weeks
at a time, it is because I would die
hopeless as a bear in a steel-jawed
trap if it could not roam free.

The Elephant in the Room

I don't want to be here, either,
bulk pinched between sofa and television,
tension an ache in my bowels. Worst
of all is being invisible, the man's
anger prodding my flank like a sharp stick,
the woman's sorrow chaining my legs
to the hardwood floor. If ignored much
longer, I fear I will go mad, yank
the iron pegs from the floor, rip the stick
from the man's cruel hands with my muscular
trunk. But I am immobilized by their
denial, have no more substance than
a gray cloud of moisture and gas that
threatens thunder and lightning but
delivers only a dull and steady rain.

The Need to Believe

We'd love to believe we're not
like other animals, red in tooth
and claw, but the evening news
belies us. Our teeth are bullets,
our claws shrapnel bombs,
homemade and manufactured.

We'd love to believe that God
reached down and plucked us
from the wild pack, designating
us his representatives on earth.
But my vote goes to mountains
and the fields of daisies at their feet.

We'd love to believe that death
can be fooled, that soft clouds, virgins,
and eternal life await us. But all this
smacks of vivid imagination.
We'd love to believe we're special,
that our lives impress the earth.

But earth has trees that live
for centuries, hidden places
we will never see; she forgets us
as quickly as raindrops
evaporate on hot stone.

The Former Pianist

Enslaved to the ebony monster
by her parents at an age
when she could barely distinguish
her own desires from theirs,
she served it well, if miserably,
for decades. Hounded by ever more

demanding teachers, she wrung from it
and from herself the complex
tonalities of Hindemuth,
the brutally frequent notes of Liszt.
The lyricism of Brahms provided
some relief, but not enough.

She dreamed of being crushed
by the piano, its dark hulk
bearing down on her frail bones
until they cracked. Finally,
at forty, she's had enough

of black and white keys dancing
demonically beneath her fingers,
playing her more than she played them.
Now in dreams she slams the keyboard cover
down upon her teacher's grasping
hands, for once hearing

his bones crack instead of hers.
Her tiny feet shove the high-strung
mass of the piano off the edge
of the stage, leave it
listing on a broken leg,
strings humming furiously.

Malibu, December 2008

The tide is out. I stand on mud flats,
gazing back toward shore. My daughter,
her back to me, steps carefully from
one seaweed-covered rock to another
as she returns to the beach. Her arms,
half lifted for balance, give her the look
of a bird about to take flight.

Her brother, a few years younger, waits
ahead, hands in pockets, eyes blue-green
as the ocean, Carhartt hoodie
clay-brown like the cliffs beyond.
Both wear jeans rolled up to the knee,
the exposed skin of their calves
pink-white as a baby's.

The sea loves the shore. The tide returns.
Soft, incoming waves wash over me
bearing messages from a vast sea.

Ping Pong with Henry Miller

At the author's rustic library in Big Sur
my twenty-year-old son Charlie and I
play on the warped table outside.
I score easily, my shots skidding off detritus
from redwoods, which stand like lingam
honoring Miller's insatiable libido.
Miller was an aggressive ping pong player,
too, enjoyed the give and take, the high curves
and deep thrusts. Charlie hasn't discovered
Miller yet, but I understand the stakes.
My own libido has cooled, while his
burns hot. Here, I can send a young man
packing, pretend that my prowess
with a little white ball matters.

PAPER BOY

Paper Boy, 1962

I wade into darkness that takes my
breath away, canvas bag burdened
with murders, avalanches, famine,
racial violence. The strap cuts
into my shoulder like an instrument
of torture. I scan the street for
territorial dogs, half-expect
horror movie creatures to emerge
from between houses. I find courage
in the rhythm: walk, throw, walk, throw,
climb the steep suburban hill to
road's end, where the wide tank of an
enormous silver water tower looms
like a flying saucer. I am a boy
made of paper, shredded by fear
of stray animals, aliens, atom
bombs, eighth-grade bullies, the threat of
eternal damnation. And, yet, when dawn lifts
the curtain from the streets of Whitefish Bay,
blushing light lures me back on stage
to imagine a life that's front page news.

Gods

After my paper route, I turned to
comic books, brightly inked newsprint
with muscular heroes and full-breasted
heroines, the flashing of claws, fists,
light rays, the swift, sure dealing of
justice and revenge. My favorite

was Thor, he of the massive chest,
eighteen-inch biceps and long yellow hair,
wielding the hammer of the gods to
obliterate human evil, crushing
villains' skulls, hurling bolts of lightning
into their strongholds. His being a pagan

god added zest to the experience,
time off from my all-seeing, all-knowing,
ethereal God. Thor was Jesus
on steroids, not just turning over
the moneychangers' tables but hurling them
into the sun to burn like matchsticks.

I'd have liked to see the Romans try to crucify
Thor. He'd have snapped their cross in two,
picked his teeth with the splinters. Thor was
a blast of lusty energy to counter
the pale, black-robed priests who didn't know
one end of a hammer from the other
or a god from a flat-faced mosaic
pressed into a church wall.

Born Again

Kennedy, the headline blared, would challenge
any Russian ship bearing rockets for Castro.
In school, we'd practiced ducking under desks,
trouped en masse into the thick-walled church
basement, the threat of nuclear attack
palpable as the threat of thunderstorms—
we scanned the sky for enemy bombers
instead of clouds. That morning
on my paper route the air was clear
and quiet. In the cul de sac, a street
with no exit, I happened to look up,
saw a contrail higher than I'd ever
seen before, antiseptic white against
the cold blue sky. For a few long minutes
I tasted the metallic flavor of death
falling from a perfect sky,
murmured an Act of Contrition,
held my breath…until the bomber
passed far out over Lake Michigan.
I breathed again, a breath sweeter
than the first breath of summer vacation,
when life smells of sunlight and possibility.

Collecting

The paper boy goes door to door, collecting
payment for the daily news, for horoscopes
and weather, want ads and comic strips, advice
on love and home improvement. He finds his
customers cutting lawns, making dinner

or swimming in the blue glow of TV.
No one likes to pay, but his being a boy
makes it easier. While a diapered child
stares at him through a screen door, a woman
fetches her purse. With a dog barking behind him,

a man peels off an extra dollar, yells
"Shut up, Rusty!" over his shoulder.
The boy is shy of interrupting them,
but enjoys voyeuristic glimpses into
lives of people still asleep when he

walks his route, their dark morning
houses opening like colorful flowers.
Mrs. Schneider wears a wig and purple
housecoat all day, the Firer's high school
daughter sunbathes in red on the front lawn,

his classmate Kathy invites him in
to suck on bright Popsicles. At Christmastime
they hand him envelopes with a five or ten,
just reward, he feels, for plowing through snow
and dark, fighting for balance on icy walks,

enduring eyeball-freezing cold. They don't
let him forget that he's a servant,
complaining when the paper's late or wet
or when the price goes up, but, still,
they have to pay him when he comes.
They owe him.

Crypt of St. Francis, Assisi, Italy

It is dark as the secrets
of the Catholic Church. No birds
flit gaily about, as they
do on his holy cards.
Only dim light settles
on our shoulders. Down here
I'm drawn to thoughts of his self-
flagellation, his whips
of nails and leather,
his disdain for the poor
donkey of his body, which he
tried to beat into submission.

But the flesh is brave and pagan,
will endure countless false
lessons to teach us one that's true.
Even Francis apologized
to his lacerated body
on his deathbed, before the Church
consigned him to this dim sepulcher
and the bloodless fame of sainthood.

Bombed in Las Vegas

*In the early 1950s, people in Las Vegas sat on casino
rooftops all night to watch early morning nuclear
explosions at the Nevada Test Site 65 miles away.*

Zombie was the drink of choice as we awaited
the explosion, all night on the rooftop
of the Sands, sports jackets buttoned, shawls wrapped
tight against the cold and brittle desert air.

We would have preferred martinis,
but the girls insisted we drink with them,
and these were girls we wanted to please, hoping
they'd please us come morning.

We'd seen bombs explode before, Al and I,
all up and down the length of Europe,
but Artie, testing A-bombs down the road
told us, "You ain't seen nothin' yet, my friends!"

By the time dawn appeared, a knife edge
on the horizon, Joe was dueling tongues
with Doris, my hand was far up Sally's skirt.
And then the thing exploded.

The rumble was like a million tanks rolling
across France, the wind like as many bombers
whooshing overhead, the light as if
the earth itself were a cannon muzzle.

And as the monstrous cloud began to rise
like nothing less than Death himself,
I crawled into Sally's welcome lap
and buried my fear in her perfume.

Later, we made love like animals, proving
we, at least, were still alive, unlike the Japs
at Hiroshima and Nagasaki,
who suddenly could have been next door.

46 § *Before Whose Glory*

Drinks at The Blue Goose

It was as near to drinking,
that adult rite of passage,
as we could get as boys, when
our father, Major Kessenich,
a stern or playful man
by turns, escorted us to the
officers' club at Camp McCoy,
showing us off like a proud
gander at The Blue Goose.

As we walked, enlisted men
passing in open jeeps or
crunching along white gravel
paths between barracks saluted
Dad, who took it as his due,
saluting them back without
breaking stride, while we puffed out
our chests, saluting, too, our
egos big as howitzers.

The Blue Goose was dim inside.
Our entrance sent a blaze
of sunlight across the
polished floor. The handful of
officers gathered at that
early hour looked up and smiled.
The bartender, a balding
sergeant with a gold tooth, boomed,
"What's your pleasure, gentlemen?"

Our pleasure was ginger ale—
and being there among the men
in uniform as they whacked
their brown leather dice cup on
the burnished bar, played cribbage,
and caught themselves about to

swear, unspoken words
hanging in the air like the
girlie calendar on the wall.

The sergeant poured our drinks in
highball glasses just like Dad's,
cold golden bubbles rising
to the top and clinging to
the ice cubes like diamonds—
a drink that looked exactly like
champagne, the drink of those
who have everything they want.

Trying to Save Jackie Kennedy

It is 1960, on the campaign trail.
We sit across a folding table from
each other at Jack's headquarters
in Milwaukee. I am no longer
ten, but twenty, old enough to
notice Jackie's feline tongue dart
across the envelopes that she is
licking ceremoniously
for the cameras, the dutiful
wife, while Jack screws a volunteer
in the restroom. Jackie's widespread
eyes meet mine, she smiles, and I know
she will come home to my modest
studio apartment, sunglasses hiding
those famous eyes. Once there, she is
as calm and sweet as I've imagined
she would be, complimenting
my bad LaTrec and Van Gogh
prints, allowing me to take her
gently on the mattress on my floor.
"Leave Jack," I say when we are through.
"He's bad for you." But she just laughs
that tinkling laugh, which will soon be
broadcast nationwide as she leads
us on a tour of the White House.
Then she stretches like a cat,
gets up, dresses slowly, unself-
consciously, as I watch her from
the floor. She leans down to kiss me
on the forehead, then steps outside
into the blazing sun, boards
the funereal limousine.

Generation Gap

She was born at Woodstock
and her parents never fail
to tell the story. "Right there
in the meadow in the pouring
rain!" they say. The years
have added thunder, lightning
and a Santa Claus-like
hippie handing out cigar-
sized joints to celebrate.

She never tells anyone.
It does nothing for
her credibility. She told
a college boyfriend once,
a musician who would have
sucked the blood from her veins
to get closer to the Sixties.
As her parents might say,
it freaked her out.

They still live in a cabin
in Vermont. Their compost heap,
outhouse and scruffy goats
embarrass her, even when she's alone.
And if she brings a friend along,
her parents inevitably
play the Woodstock album
and haul out their dog-eared
photographs, in which they see
rain-drenched, tie-dyed people
celebrating freedom, love and joy.
All she sees are pigs in the mud,
and herself, a pink piglet
squealing in protest.

Pig 'n' Whistle

On learning that my high school hangout
is being replaced with a nursing home.

"The Pig," where, in our raucous youth,
we gorged on burgers big as two fists,
now welcomes us back with meat cut
into tiny, chewable pieces.
The drive where hoods paraded
their muscle cars is replaced
by hallways where they roll walkers
fast as scrawny legs can carry them.
Where once boys pressed pretty girls
against brick walls, nurses
insert catheters. The bloom
and glow of healthy flesh gives way
to gray skin and sagging asses.

We did not see this coming.

We ate Ballpark Special sundaes,
oblivious of diabetes, feasted
on Big Chief burgers, not foreseeing
cholesterol counts as high as
batting averages. And when we led
girls into the dark back seats of cars
we could not imagine one day being
led into the dim lounge of a
Sunrise Senior Living Center by
a candy striper, deposited on a bench
to stare quietly into the night.

BEAUTY ON THE BUS

Beauty on the Bus

She caresses soft pink onto
the pale, delicate skin of her cheeks,
chin and forehead with a sable brush,

coyly tilting her head from side
to side to swing long
strawberry hair from her

face. I see her eyes in the mirror.
She sees only herself, brushing
blush on high cheekbones

just so. She moves
on to mascara, twirling the
spiral brush through her impossibly

long lashes, making them even
longer. She balances this effect
with eyeliner, punctuating her

bright green eyes with a fine, unwavering
line, despite the bounce and jostle
of the bus beneath her. She finishes

with a hint of shadow, carefully
matched to her eyes, which now
stand out like pools of seawater.

They say a man can drown
in an inch of water if he
falls into it, loses consciousness.

I imagine tumbling into those
wet, green eyes, taking leave
of my senses, dying happily.

Falling in Love with Roma

She hums like a Vespa,
persistent, gentle and
serpentine in her
movements. Beside her,
New York is a thug
on a motorcycle,
L.A. a waif with
bleached hair and dirt
on her nose. Roma is
elegant and easy,
a princess in jeans
with rubies at her throat,
a socialite in evening
dress lifting her skirt
to step into a fountain.
She eats well, at her
leisure, too much in love
with tastes tantalizing
her palate to deny
herself—and for the same
reason disinclined to
gluttony. Three days
with her were not enough,
and though she is too
worldly, too self-possessed
to miss me, I will long
for her until the day
her arms enfold me
once again.

Victorian Painting

The girl in the foreground is mute
as the gray stump of house behind her.
Something pushes out from behind her face,
enlarges her ears, expands her head.
Her hat no longer fits. It lies
discarded on the lawn, red ribbon trailing.
Her parents have not moved for an hour.
The mother is sheathed in black,
the father in Sunday best.
The cat near the pram is not a cat at all;
it is a stone. Nor is the sheep alive.
It must have wandered into the yard
and froze. Nothing moves here,
though the girl may try. The hill
beneath her feet is a gripped fist.

Soccer Mom's Lament

Families that move into McMansions sometimes
become so atomized that they need family therapy
to recover.
> —Heard in NPR interview

I lost Willie somewhere on the third floor.
Mina goes to the basement and disappears
for weeks. My husband Karl practically lives
in the home theater, watching fourteen
channels of sports on a screen the size of
a garage door. Half the time, I don't even
know when they get home. They're like
guests returning to a motel, parking
half a block from the front desk. I stay near
the kitchen, where each of them must come
to graze, eventually, even when
they beg off meals. They arrive from their
respective lairs glaze-eyed, like animals
emerging from the forest at night,
and while they browse our acres of
refrigerator, freezer and shelf space,
I catch them up on family news
and extract a few words about
what's going on, what they need, and when
I might enjoy the privilege of seeing them again.

The Invasion of Italy

I watch our olive-skinned boys lean against
the wall, intent upon a German woman
unfolding her long, white, mini-skirted legs
from a Mercedes. She slips off her sunglasses,

nests them in her golden hair, exposing
eyes the blue of summer evening skies.
I marvel at these Northern women, creatures
of ice who carry in their bodies sun and light.

She walks like a Teutonic princess to the
fountain (a walk I later try to imitate),
bends over—every boy leaning with her—opens
her frosted lips and sips a pure stream of water
from the marble O of a satyr's mouth.

She drinks her fill, wipes her chin, and smiles at her
admirers. "Shotze," calls Gino ("sweetheart"—
the only German word he knows). Paolo coos,
"Hey, baby." She does not reply, just lifts

the sunglasses from her hair and covers her eyes
as a cloud blots out the sun. Vito whimpers,
Giani bites his fist. I imagine what it must
feel like to watch boys fall at your sandaled feet.

Indifferent to their pain (and mine) she folds herself
back into the Mercedes, with one more flash
of thigh, and is gone. Just as, inevitably,
a BMW glides in, and its door swings open.

Mail, Female

They sit side-by-side in a lonely corner
of the parking lot: his boxy white
Postal Service van, her fiery orange
Subaru pickup. It's not as if
he's a perfect match for her—God knows
no one looks good in that uniform—
but he delivers dependably.
("Neither rain, nor snow, nor heat…")
It excites her to fuck him
on top of the mail bags in the back
of the truck, supported by the
dense weight of love letters, birthday cards,
utility bills, bank account statements,
and "Dear John" letters. She knows she ought to
write him the latter, leave her truck parked
in the carport, sort through her own bills,
but when the mail drops through her slot
at noon her body quickens, remembering
the rough feel of canvas on her back
as he enters her, the pressure of
small boxes in the bags as he
presses down.

Suicide of a Socialite

After a photo by Weegee

If suicide were this
beautiful, we'd all
have tried it.
The car roof, indented
by the impact of her
body, cradles her. She
wears an evening
gown and looks serene.
Bits of windshield
surround her like
diamonds interred
with a princess.
There is no telling
what drove her to leap,
but it no longer matters.
Some would say she
was ruled by darkness,
but she is the ruler now.
She rests in state forever,
her bier a shattered
automobile, her line
of mourners stretching
far into the future.

In the K-Mart Lot

I call these shoppers grander
than a herd of elk on a white plain,
a school of salmon surging upriver.
The stooped man pushing his walker
by baby steps toward the sliding door
took out a machine gun nest at Anzio
to save his brothers' lives. The woman
with the wild, hennaed hair and rolled down
stockings ran off to Broadway to dance.
The tattooed delivery boy pays his
drunken mother's rent and tucks her
into bed each night. A magnificent
rack of antlers, the drive to leap dams
are gifts unearned, but the people exposed
on this unforgiving blacktop chose
their challenges. I'll put their bellows
of defiance up against an elk's call any day,
trump the determination of a salmon
with their "Yes, I will."

Wild Turkeys

I watch them from my office window
pecking at pebbles on the blacktop,
pink heads, iridescent feathers,
stick legs moving with surprising grace.

Living in the woods behind the office
park, they tolerate our diurnal presence,
unmoved by creatures four times their size
invading in steel and glass.

Ben Franklin preferred them for our national
symbol, and they act as if they deserve no less.

How different would our nation be if we
had chosen these gentle grazers—who
nonetheless defend their nests—over
a bird who scours the earth for prey?

American though they are, these turkeys have
no allegiance. They only need a patch of earth
to scratch, a place to raise their pink young. And,
come to think of it, do any of us need more?

Your Rome, My Rome

My wife see ranks of phallic
columns thrusting skyward,
dominating everything.

I notice the columns'
broken tops softened by wind
and rain and sun, the sinuous
vines creeping up their sides.

My wife hears Roman legions
tramping off to kill, maim
and subject. But I

hear sputtering motorbikes
bumping over ancient
stones with laughing women
clinging to their men.

She imagines gladiators
bathed in gore. But even
at the Coliseum
sweet grass carpets the
killing fields and feminine
arches frame blue skies.

Blue Yonder

Copilot Loses It, Seeks God at 30,000 Feet
—*Boston Metro* headline

All his life, they assured him
God was up there. He became a pilot
to get closer. Year after year, he saw
blank sky, unblinking sun, stars

sparkling like tears in the night.
His yearning became unbearable.
He begged God to speak with him.
It seemed so little to ask. One day,

as he flew above clouds soft
as angel wings, he asked God
out loud in the cockpit. The pilot
tried to calm him, but he began to shout,

"I have a right to speak with You! I am
as much Your creature as Moses or
Mohammed, who spoke with You
so often. I deserve to be heard!"

He came to, shackled in the economy section,
the seats on either side of him empty,
passengers across the aisle staring,
afraid he would start ranting again,

but he was exhausted, heart broken into
a galaxy of pieces. Then a face appeared
above the seat in front of him, round, mischievous,
a two-year-old haloed in red hair.

All she did was look at him—no fear
or judgment in her startling blue eyes.
All she did was look at him and see
that he was there.

Green Tea

The secret, he said, was green tea—
a man could drink all night if he
had "green tea and a variety
of snacks." It seemed to work for me,
too, though I was a woman and
half his weight. Not that I ever
tested his theory anywhere
but in that dingy living room.

A Chinese girl had taught him,
he said, that year he'd gone to college,
never to return. "She could drink
anyone under the table, and
nobody could figure out how."
Jack had seduced her
to uncover her secret, then
dropped her like so many others.

His snacks tended toward the
exotic: wasabi peas that
burned the lining of my nose,
crackers made with kelp, salmon
mousse dip—foods I never ate
anywhere but at Jack's house.
Nor did I drink elsewhere the
way I did with him—whole bottles
of whiskey, gin or scotch between

us as we talked till dawn about
my father—his brother, the
successful lawyer—married to
just one woman, while Jack had gone
through five; about the symbolism
in *The Rainbow,* our favorite book;
or about how to grow a
marijuana plant that loves you back.

It was Jack who'd given me
my first cigarette, my first drink
my first joint, my first
banned books. It was Jack who'd
advised me to play the field,
saved me from a pallid life
as Mrs. Connor Pennington—
a debt I can never repay.

So, it is I alone who
visit him, sitting on a sofa
that kicks up dust at the slightest
touch, amid lamps with 15-watt
bulbs to save his eyes. The others
he owes money or a wife or
an apology. Me he owes
nothing but green tea and crackers.

Existentialism Revisited

Full of Mexican food and margaritas
at sunset we wander down to a public deck
overlooking Lake Champlain. The Adirondacks
across the still water, one rank behind the other
like cardboard mountains in a children's play,
turn blue and pink and gray as the sun descends.

Below, pleasure boats dock at a lakeside
restaurant, a toddler in red shorts clatters
across the weathered gray planks, and a
terrier sits alert at the foot of his master's
deck chair. Sailboats, sails reefed,
glide into the harbor, running lights aglow

like candles floating down a river.
I inhale the pleasing scent of lake water.
My daughter rests her pretty head on
my shoulder while my son folds himself
to lean on the railing and gaze out
at the light show on the horizon.

Redolent air cups us in its
gentle palm, as if we were precious
jewels—and who's to say we are not?
Our consciousness graces this planet.
We are the eyes of God, the consumers
of Creation, and if we sometimes gorge

ourselves at the feast, who can blame us?
The eyes see, the ears hear, the fingers touch,
the nose smells, the tongue tastes. Most
importantly, the heart feels, welling up
like a late summer watermelon—pink, ripe,
fat with the sweet juice of existence.

BLAZING HEART

The Cathedral of Justo Gallepo

I limit myself to the offering every day of work
which He chooses to cede to me and to feel happy
with what I have achieved so far.
                                        —Justo Gallepo

For more than four decades, he has hauled
corrugated iron, discarded
construction bricks, bags of gravel, clay
and cement to the piece of land his parents
left him. Working alone, or with a few
volunteers, without permits or
architectural knowledge, he has raised
archways, cloister, spiral staircase,
portico and a striking blue dome
one hundred thirty feet into the air.
But he is far from done. Inside, rusted
scaffolding stretches precariously
upward toward the incomplete roof. Justo,
still spry at eighty-one, lifts his materials
heavenward with the help of a
bicycle wheel pulley, following them
up with the agility of a monkey.

Some come to laugh at him, as if he were
in a zoo, but others stand in awe of
his accomplishment, his devotion
to the Virgin Mary, for whom a rough bench
turned altar has been covered with prayer cards,
statues and candles weeping wax.
An immense wooden collection box
contains monetary tributes to his
perseverance. For forty years, since being
expelled from a Trappist monastery
with tuberculosis, Justo has built
onto his cathedral. From the crypt to
the soaring dome, he has poured his heart
and soul into a building no one wants.

"It's just a pity he didn't try to build
something more useful," says the barman
wiping glasses across the street. "We have
enough churches." But Justo builds
not for neighbors, nor even for himself.
He pours each backbreaking bucket of
cement, puts each broken piece of brick
into place, for the glory of Almighty God
and Mary, the human mother of Jesus,
before whose glory the cries of "fool"
fade to inaudible whispers.

The Sacrifice

*...then one of the peat-bog cutters digs up
the man...head squashed like a pumpkin.*
—Seamus Heaney

To us it seems barbaric, crushing
a man's skull to bring on spring.
But if I were that man, honored
among all of my tribe, fed with milk
and honey, certain of the hour
and purpose of my death, I believe
I would dream of water flowing
from the sky, wheat bursting
from the earth where my body
lay, feeding my people and
inscribing, for at least one season,
my name upon their bellies and hearts.

The Life of a Tree

For a decade, my neighbor's
linden sang me a hallelujah
every morning, dependable
as the sunrise. Leafed or leafless,
its branches extended at
perfect angles toward the sky
like the arms of a gospel choir
reaching for paradise. It was a
wakeup call, a morning prayer,
a song of innocence.

That day, in its hallowed place
an immense hole hovered in the air.
Below lay wood chips
spattered like blood on the lawn.
My neighbor, it seems, had tired
of the tree, cut it down, limb by limb.
Now, each Halloween, a figure
of the Grim Reaper rises
on the stump, skull shrunken
beneath a black hood, scythe lifted
skyward at a wicked angle.

But still the tree hovers there,
phantom limbs reaching
over the roof, its absence
more disturbing than some
party store figure of death, its spirit
undaunted by the chainsaw
wielding neighbor, who only
thought he had the power to kill.

Underground Jesus

What if Jesus had sprung from the ground like a sapling,
and when he left burrowed back into the earth, returning
to a heaven marked by glorious stalagmites?

Instead of all this rising up, this disappearing
into clouds and blinding light, we'd have saints with shovels,
avatars in diamond mines, bodhisattvas with arms
wrapped happily around the dark roots of trees.

Did volcanoes convince us to put hell below the ground,
seething fire, belching smoke, smelling of scorched earth,
while we worshipped the sun—which burns as readily as
it nurtures? Earth holds more than fire, dispenses life

as freely as the sun. It, too, giveth and taketh away. And, yet,
we call sky "the heavens" while we abuse the earth.
We launch into the blue our saints, our hopes, our probes,
know more about the depths of space than our own planet's core.

Perhaps when he returns to judge the living and the dead,
Christ will eschew fiery cloud, burning hail, and come as Jesus,
the man, rising black and angry from an oil-soaked lake.

Blazing Heart

The blazing heart of Jesus
in the gaudy print
on the dark living room wall
frightened him most of all.
He sat pressed against the sofa arm
close to the end table with
the painted plaster statue of Mary
holding baby Jesus. His own
mother was traveling
the world with his siblings,
while he'd been dumped
on their Irish cleaning woman
who lived behind closed shades,
summer barely sneaking in
around the edges. The only

saving grace was Saturday
night in the vast tiled space
of Miami Cathedral
where he could trade his family's
stark Presbyterianism
for Catholicism's
sensual delights, dip his
fingers into cool holy water,
fill his eyes with jeweled
stained glass and life-sized statues,
breathe in the exotic sweetness
of incense and beeswax candles that
made the air itself glow.

When the Mass commenced
the choir burst into
joyous song, the priest entered
in colorful robes, preceded
by his acolytes, mounted
the steps to the altar,

chanted Latin incantations
like a magician, eventually
raised the golden cup, turning
the wine, she whispered to him,
into Jesus's blood,
the bright white host
into His body, which
the boy was not privileged to eat.

He returned home exhausted
from the pageantry, face flushed
with excitement. In bed, he lay
on his back in thin pajamas,
covers kicked off in the heat,
clutching in his sweaty fist
a plastic figurine of the Mother
of God the cleaning woman
had given him, imagining
his own mother as she traveled
further and further away.

Checkout Justice

When he ran out of jurors for a trial, an Ohio judge sent sheriff's deputies to the local Wal-Mart to issue summonses to surprised shoppers.

I was standing at the checkout counter
in the grocery section, my hand extended
for change, when the deputy slapped the summons
into it, grinning like a frat boy playing
a practical joke. Others were served over
watermelons or along with a pound
of burger at the deli counter.

Twenty of us were led to an old school bus,
allowed only to put our groceries in our cars,
leaving lettuce to wilt in its bag, ice cream
to melt into soup. Like criminals, we
could make one call. I told my wife
to eat lunch without me, if she could find
anything in the refrigerator.

The deputies informed us it was a big trial,
that, if chosen, we might be sequestered.
I thought of bananas rotting in my trunk.
The judge was a bilious old man with pastry
crumbs down the front of his robe. He whipped
the lawyers with his sharp voice until they
chose enough shoppers to fill out the jury.

And then it was over, for those not chosen.
Dropped back at the Wal-Mart lot, it was as if
we'd stepped outside for a long cigarette break.
We could have continued shopping—all night
if we'd wanted to—but who knew where we might
end up if we dawdled at the dairy case
or took too long to grind our coffee.

Fragile

Glass delusion is the belief that all or part of one's
body has turned to glass.
　　　　　　　　—*Boston Globe* article

His hands are not replicas, science museum displays
with ice-chip fingernails, pipettes curved into veins
beneath transparent skin. Their glass is deep blue, like the hand
of Krishna waving to his followers. He imagines followers, too,
protecting his delicate fingers from the sharp protrusions
of daily life, the railings, park benches, and hastily closed doors.
You, of the meat hands, have no idea. Skin and flesh grow back,
but glass, once broken, is reparable only in the crudest way.
Those with broken hands beg on the streets, like lepers in India,
their jagged digits frightening away all but the most compassionate.
He needs his protective entourage but fears they tire of him. One day,
he will release them with an act of love, free his frangible hands
from their padding, raise them high above his head, and bring them
down on a concrete wall, shattering them into pieces of night sky.

The Piano

In May, 2006, workers at the 4,406-foot
summit of Ben Nevis in Scotland, the tallest
mountain in the British Isles, found a piano.

Draft horse and cart could only get
the old man's piano so far
up the mountainside. Then it took
the sweat and blood of a dozen
hired men, cursing every step
all day in the midsummer sun.
Blair MacCallum snapped his femur,
bone protruding white as the summit
of Ben Nevis in winter. He was
carried away and another
took his place, wrapping the fat leg
of the old man's Bosendorfer
in his arms as if it were a
child from hell. More than once, the men
threatened to quit, leave the black
hulk listing on the mountainside,
but the thick gold coins the old man had
flashed before them in the cool
morning air spurred them on.

They were astonished when they made it,
half expecting the thing to slide
back down the mountainside like the rock
of Sisyphus. But it was on
flat ground and would never move again.
The old man, who had been carried
up the steep slope on his bench,
was set before the piano, beaming
like a child on Christmas Eve.
And as he began to play, the
notes of a Beethoven sonata

surging on the summer breeze, the
sunset sky blazing pink and gray,
the exhausted men removed their hats
and, one by one, sank to their knees.

Acknowledgments

The author would like to thank the following publisher and magazines for publishing his work, often in slightly different form:

The Atlanta Review: "The Invasion of Italy"
Sewanee Review: "Drinks at the Blue Goose," "Blazing Heart,"
    "Natural Progression"
Poetry Ireland Review: "Angelus." The author would also like to thank
    the Strokestown International Poetry Festival judges, Enda Wyley,
    Julie O'Callaghan and Sebastian Barker, for awarding the festival's
    €4,000 first prize to this poem.
Chronogram (reprinted in *New Millennium Writers*): "Bombed in
    Las Vegas"
Passager: "Paper Boy, 1962," "Rebirth," "Collecting" (as parts I, IV & VI
    of a longer poem)
Ekleksographia: "Fragile," "The Elephant in the Room"
Ibbetson Street: "In the K-Mart Lot," "Falling in Love with Roma," "Gods"
Somerville News: "General Grandma"
Sackbut Review: "Victorian Painting"
Word Riot: "Check Out Justice"
Wilderness House Literary Review: "Blue Yonder," "Wild Turkeys,"
    "Check-Out Justice"
Soul-Lit: "Enlightenment"
Spirit First Anthology: "Meditating with a Dog Named Vasana"
Verse Wisconsin (nominated for a Pushcart Prize): "Underground Jesus"

Strange News, a chapbook published by Pudding House Publications in 2008, contained the following poems: "The Piano," "The Need to Believe," "Trying to Save Jackie Kennedy," "The Artisan," "Emergency Call," "Suicide of a Socialite," "Seduction," "Generation Gap," "Death Wish," "Daniel Boone Speaks to His Wife," and "Fatal Insomnia."

Finally, the author would like to thank Kathleen Spivack, Jay Weber and Diane Kistner, whose editing of poems and help with arranging them made this a better book.

Cover art, "Ceu Final de Tarde" by Luis Fernando Lima Marinho; author photo by Joseph A. Cohen; cover and interior book design by Diane Kistner

About FutureCycle Press

FutureCycle Press is dedicated to publishing lasting English-language poetry and flash fiction books, chapbooks, and anthologies in both print-on-demand and ebook formats. Founded in 2007 by long-time independent editor/publishers and partners Diane Kistner and Robert S. King, the press incorporated as a nonprofit in 2012. A number of our editors are distinguished poets and authors in their own right, and we have been actively involved in the small press movement going back to the early seventies.

The FutureCycle Poetry Book Prize and honorarium is awarded annually for the best full-length volume of poetry we publish in a calendar year. Introduced in 2013, our Good Works projects are devoted to issues of global significance, with all proceeds donated to a related worthy cause. We are dedicated to giving all authors we publish the care their work deserves, making our catalog of titles the most distinguished it can be, and paying forward any earnings to fund more great books

We've learned a few things about independent publishing over the years. We've also evolved a unique, resilient publishing model that allows us to focus mainly on vetting and preserving for posterity the most books of exceptional quality without becoming overwhelmed with bookkeeping and mailing, fundraising activities, or taxing editorial and production "bubbles." To find out more about what we are doing, come see us at www.futurecycle.org.

Made in the USA
San Bernardino, CA
27 April 2015